YOUNG PEOPLE'S ANIMAL ENCYCLOPEDIA

Volume 2
Armadillo to Batfish

Edited by MAURICE BURTON, D. Sc.

CHILDRENS PRESS, CHICAGO

American Revised Edition Published 1980
Original American Edition Published 1969 by
Regensteiner Publishing Enterprises, Inc.
All Rights Reserved   Printed in U.S.A.
Published Simultaneously in Canada

© Alberto Peruzzo Editore and Studio Creazioni Dami

1 2 3 4 5 6 7 8 9 10 11 12 13 14 15 16 17 18 19 20 21 22 23 24 25 R 86 85 84 83 82 81

Pichiciego or fairy armadillo *(Chlamyphorus truncatus)*

Scientists know that armadillos are very sensitive to ground vibrations. These vibrations warn an armadillo that a possible enemy is approaching. To escape its enemies, the armadillo will burrow underground quickly, leaving nothing above ground to show of his presence but a small pile of dirt.

ARMADILLO, FAIRY

The most unusual of the armadillos is the six-inch **pichiciego** or **fairy armadillo** of the western Argentine. This has an armour, as in other armadillos, but with a difference. Its body is covered with long, soft white fur, almost like silk. Over its back is an armour of 20 pink horny plates but this is attached only to the spine, so that it is no more than a loose cover over the back. The hind end of the body is flat and bears its own shield of horny plates. Not only is the pichiciego shaped like a mole, it also lives underground, seldom venturing above ground, but when it does it risks being taken by a predator such as the ocelot. The pichiciego is said to retreat into its tunnel at the first alarm, and to block the entrance to enemies with its own flattened and armoured hindquarters.

ARMADILLO, GIANT

One of the world's strangest looking animals is the **giant armadillo** of the Brazilian forests, which is completely encased in armour. A member of an ancient race whose history goes back about seventy-million years, it looks like a war tank created centuries before man invented that modern mobile fortress. The one-hundred pound body of the giant armadillo is covered with hard, bony plates, which fit together just like pieces of armour, giving it both a protection which is almost impenetrable, and a flexibility which allows it to scuttle about easily. If the wary giant armadillo should sense an enemy approaching it will burrow into the earth with a speed that is little short of astonishing, leaving only a pile of loose earth to greet its enemy. Measuring nearly five feet from its pointed nose to the tip of its shell-encased tail, it bustles across forest floors with ease, in its continual search for insects. It will dig them out with the stout claws of its forefeet like a miniature bulldozer. And as it digs, it mops up colonies of insects with a few quick thrusts of its tongue, which is almost as long as that of its close relative, the anteater. Although not very beautiful, the giant armadillo conceals beneath its coat-of-mail some of the tastiest flesh eaten by the South American Indians, who say it is as delicious as a young roast pig.

Giant armadillo *(Priodontes giganteus)*

Ugly on the outside, armadillos, large and small, are hunted by both animals and humans for their meat. Cooked armadillo meat tastes much like roast pig.

ARMADILLO, HAIRY

The **peludo** prefers to escape from its enemies by burrowing into the loose soil of the Argentine pampas, using its hard head and clawed

Peludo or hairy armadillo (*Chaetophractus villosus*)

rivers, streams and deserts, into a large part of the southern and south-western United States. Water does not bother it, but there are two ways of crossing it. If the stream is narrow, the armadillo simply holds its breath, plunges in, scurries across the river bed, and toddles onto land. For wider rivers it gulps air into its intestine, to give itself buoyancy, and then swims at the surface. The yellowish-brown nine-banded armadillo is completely encased in a dome-shaped shell which leaves no part of its body unprotected. Its armour is made of small bony plates covered with horn, forming shields over its fore- and hindquarters, and nine separate hinged bands across its back, which give it its name. Although so well-protected the long-clawed nine-banded armadillo digs at least eight different burrows, some thirteen feet deep, into which to retreat. During the day it slumbers in one of these, but every night comes out to hunt for insects with its long, pig-like snout.

toes to do the digging. It will, however, use its other form of protection also for attack. This consists of a bony shell on the fore- and hindquarters, with six hinged bands between. Since tufts of hair grow between the joints of these bands, the animal has been called peludo, the hairy one. Though mainly an eater of insects and clover, the armadillo is capable of becoming a real killer. It will approach a mouse by racing back and forth, and will not start its attack until it has pinpointed its quarry. Then it halts and takes up a sitting position. But not for long! All too soon it will hurl itself upon its victim like an armoured car. It will rush upon a coiled snake in the same manner, all the while protected by its bony shell from the serpent's fangs. By rubbing the sharp edges of its bands upon the reptile's skin, the armadillo very quickly cuts the snake to pieces.

ARMADILLO, NINE-BANDED

Have you ever seen a picture of an armoured tank which soldiers can drive right into a river, across the river bottom, and onto land again? The **nine-banded armadillo** is the animal kingdom's version of just such an amphibious tank. Starting from Mexico about eighty years ago, the three-foot long, armour-encased nine-banded armadillo has migrated north across

Nine-banded armadillo (*Dasypus novemcinctus*)

ARMADILLO, THREE-BANDED

Looking like a mechanical toy that someone has just wound up and set moving, the little **peba** or **three-banded armadillo** runs across the Argentine Pampas on its hind feet, only the tips of its front claws touching the earth for balance. Suddenly it stops, turns, and eagerly heads for the tall grass to feast on a newly-found delicacy – carrion meat well-sprinkled with maggots. With its long-clawed front feet it rips the meat and devours it, grubs and all.

Peba or three-banded armadillo

(Tolypeutes tricinctus)

Known also as "Naranga" because of its pale amber colour, the little peba can roll itself into a ball about the size and shape of a small melon. Even its head and tail fit neatly into the triangular space left open by the curve of its body, almost as if it were constructed like a Chinese puzzle. When fully rolled up it is safe from most of its enemies. The jaguar and maned wolf, however, can take the armadillo in their jaws and crack its shell like a nut.

ASCALAPHID

The **ascalaphids** are natives of the tropics, but are also to be found in southern Europe and in the United States, fluttering around, sometimes in large numbers, over flower-filled meadows in search of insects smaller than themselves. They are rarely to be found in wooded areas, preferring open spaces for their swift-winged pursuit of prey. They lay their eggs in rows on plant stems, and the larvae which come out of them are flattened and fat-bodied with the characteristic long widespread jaws of the family. They feed on insects, which they seize and puncture with their mandibles, draining the body dry of blood and afterwards discarding the empty husk. The larvae are commonly found scuttling around under loose debris where they lie in wait with jaws wide open ready to snatch up whatever comes within reach. They are voracious eaters and, if given the opportunity, will readily eat even their own kind.

In their cannibalism they resemble their close relatives, the lacewing flies.

Ascalaphid *(Ascalaphidae sp.)*

ASP, EGYPTIAN

The **Egyptian asp** is found in all the countries bordering the Sahara Desert, and although food of any kind is scarce, one good meal will last it a week or more. It feeds on small rodents, birds and eggs, swallowing the latter whole. Poised above its prey, with its "hood" spread,

Egyptian asp *(Naja haje)*

Ass

it strikes, grasping its prey and "chewing" on it, so that its short, poison-bearing fangs pierce the skin in several places. The victim dies immediately, or loses consciousness, and is swallowed whole. The Egyptian asp's principal claim to fame lies in its having been smuggled to the besieged Cleopatra, as a means of her suicide and escape from capture – a reputation which it must share with the horned viper until scholars are able to agree which snake was used. At all events, it is the head of the Egyptian asp which figures so largely on Egyptian antiquities. There is only one poisonous snake in England, and this is known as the adder or viper. Its scientific name is *Vipera berus*. There are two sides to this that need explanation. First of all there is the fact that a single species should have two names, which confuses the new-comer to the study of natural history. For this we have to thank William of Normandy who conquered England in 1066. As a result of the settlement of Saxon England by the Norman French the English language is now a mixture, mainly of words derived from the Anglo-Saxon language and from the Norman-French. This often shows itself in curious ways. There is, for example, a long road in the south of England, which the Normans spoke of as the Rue, meaning street. In time the origin of the name was lost and the local people called it Rue Street. It is now known as Rew Street. This story is told merely to emphasize the dual nature of the English language. The Saxons called the poisonous snake "naedre", now corrupted to "adder". The Normans called it "viper". Later, when English-speaking naturalists travelled over the world they were inclined to call the more poisonous snakes they found by the names they knew best. Some called them adders, others called them vipers, with the result that all manner of venomous snakes have now received the common name either of adder or of viper. Sometimes we find the word "asp". The origin of this is less clear. It is from a Greek word but there is some doubt whether it was first applied to the Egyptian asp or to the horned viper of North Africa.

See Also: SNAKES

Onager (*Equus hemionus onager*)

ASS

The wild relatives of the domestic donkey range from Somaliland, in north-east Africa, to Pakistan in the east and Tibet in central Asia. They are divisible into two species, the Asiatic wild asses and the African wild asses. The first of these can be further classified into three subspecies, the second into two subspecies. For the moment we are concerned with the Asiatic wild asses. These are the **onager,** found in Persia and Afghanistan, the Indian wild ass or **ghorkar,** in Pakistan, and the **kiang** (also known as the Kulan or Chigetai), in Transcaspia

Ghorkar (*Equus hemionus khur*)

7

and Mongolia. All are desert dwellers, all are similar in appearance and habits, and all have been hunted a great deal for centuries. There used to be a wild ass in Syria and Arabia also but that is now extinct, and the three remaining subspecies are everywhere reduced in numbers. This is not on account of natural enemies because the only predators were wolves and, in some places, wild dogs. Even these hesitated to attack the adult asses, which defended themselves with their teeth and their hoofs. By lashing out with its hind hoofs a wild ass could send a wolf reeling, but the more usual form of defence is to strike downwards with the front hoofs. The tactics of wolf and dog were, therefore, to try to separate a foal from the herd. Men found similar difficulties. They found it necessary to ride down the poor beasts in parties, taking turns to chase them on horseback until the asses were exhausted. But the more profitable measures were to capture the foals, which could then be tamed and broken in. The adults were killed for their flesh and their valuable hides. All this was changed with the coming of the modern firearms. Then, in spite of the speed of the asses, as well as their natural wariness and caution, the asses stood little chance. The wild asses do not usually form large herds, partly because in desert or semi-desert country there is not the abundance of vegetation to support large numbers. These herds are composed of females and young, the adult males living apart from them, joining them only at the breeding season.

ASS, KIANG

Moving like a procession of pilgrims across the harsh tableland that includes the Tibetan plateau, Marco Polo range and the yak steppes, the herd of wild asses, known as **kiang,** seeks forage. Impervious to such different temperatures as the one hundred degree noonday heat, a freezing sunset or the teeth-chattering sub-zero weather of winter, you can find it roaming up to altitudes from 14,500 to 20,000 feet. Wild plants and grass form its daily diet, although during the rutting season its food is augmented by a special golden flower of the poppy species. It sheds its coat once a year, in the summer. At the sight of a human hunter the

kiang will flee, the members of the small herd following in single file the chief stallion. Hunters aim at this stallion because they know that the herd is lost without him. With his tremendous vitality he will still try to lead the herd out of danger even when wounded.

Kiang (*Equus hemionus kiang*)

ASS, NUBIAN WILD

There used to be a wild ass in north-west Africa, the Algerian wild ass, but this became extinct in Roman times. Farther east, the **Nubian wild ass** is today found between the Upper Nile, Ethiopia and the Red Sea. It is still there in fair numbers, but it is hunted by the local tribesmen, who eat its flesh whenever they get the opportunity. The only thing that saves the Nubian wild ass is its wariness, so that it is difficult to get near it on the flat plains where it chooses to live. At one time it was hunted on horseback and on camel, but now that the motor-car is becoming common even in those remote parts, and is being used to hunt the ass, it is a matter for doubt whether it will survive very much longer.

It is often said that there are wild asses in the Sahara, but more likely these are the descendants of domesticated asses gone wild. The fact that they can live in the Sahara shows how

Nubian wild ass *(Equus asinus africanus)*

readily asses can stand up to desert conditions. One reason is that, like the camel, an ass can go for long periods without drinking, and then, when water is plentiful, take a long drink, as much as fifteen gallons of water at a time.

ASS, NUBIAN WILD

The **Nubian wild ass** finds the lonely desert spring and has its one drink for the day. That is enough for this desert-dweller. Joining a small band of its friends, they move off across the dry and sunny African wasteland kicking up little spurts of dust. At the sparse grass of an oasis they stop to graze. Some begin to roll in the dust, grunting and snorting with pleasure as the sandy grit works itself into the back, scratching all the itches that have developed since yesterday's dust bath. When they stand and shake themselves, a cloud rises as if a very dirty rug were being beaten. After the dust settles, the distinctive black stripe on the shoulders of the Nubian ass becomes visible. One stripe runs from the base of the mane to the root of the tail. Another crosses it at shoulder-level. Legend has it that this is the "Mark of the Cross" worn by all asses as a mark of distinction because it was a donkey that carried Christ into Jerusalem on Palm Sunday. The herds of nubian asses consist of females and their young, the males joining them only at the breeding season.

Nubian wild ass

ASS, SOMALI

Centuries ago, large herds of wild asses roamed deserts and semi-deserts of north-eastern Africa. Today, these small animals are fast disappearing. The grey, four-foot high **Somali ass** is still fairly numerous in Somaliland but has been wiped out in those parts of neighbouring Ethiopia, where it used to exist. So relentlessly was it hunted for its valuable hide, which made fine leather pouches, jackets and sandals, that Ethiopian laws were passed to forbid its killing, but too late! Remarkable also for its strength and endurance, it was captured and put to use as a sturdy beast of burden. As with the other African wild ass, the Nubian, the herds are composed of females and young, the males living apart except at the breeding season.
See Also: DONKEY

ASSASSIN BUG

In every patch of weeds, the **assassin bug** moves among the leaves, searching for insect prey, piercing the soft bodies of its victims

Somali ass *(Equus asinus somalicus)*

Assassin bug *(Sinea* sp.*)*

Aye-aye *(Daubentonia madagascariensis)*

with its sharp beak, and sucking their blood. Some four thousand species of these murderous bugs lurk in the gardens of the world. One of the most familiar in the United States is the wheel-bug, so-called because of the ornamentation on its back which resembles a cog-wheel. Covered with a sticky coating, its grotesque body picks up particles of pollen, dirt and leaf litter as the insect crawls about the flowers, making an effective camouflage, aiding the assassin bug's approach to its prey. Another species, well known in the southern states, is the famous masked hunter that looks like a piece of lint as it creeps about the floors of upstairs bedrooms. Although it feeds on bed-bugs, it confronts the human inhabitants of the house with an unhappy choice, whether to endure the bites of bed-bugs or be bitten by the assassin bug.

Being bitten is not just a matter of suffering inconvenience. Some assassin bugs, transmit the germs of diseases that can, especially in the Tropics, be fatal.

AYE-AYE

Deep in the dense bamboo forests of Madagascar lives one of the world's rarest animals, the **aye-aye**. A strange squirrel-like creature with long and bony hands, this member of the Lemur family hides in secret places in the forests where the insect grubs and bamboo on which it feeds are plentiful. In the daytime, it sleeps, only emerging during the cool evening hours to forage for food. Like many of the other inhabitants of this tropical island, the aye-aye makes use of the traveller's tree. This remarkable tree provides food, drink and shelter for humans and animals alike. The local people use the palm leaves to thatch their huts, drink the pure water stored in its leaf stalks and eat its seeds. The aye-aye, too, selects the palm leaves to build the large spherical nest where the female can raise her young.

See Also: LEMUR

AZARA'S DOG

Going at a good pace, its nose to the ground like a foxhound, **Azara's dog** stops suddenly, raises its head and sniffs the wind, perhaps to check for enemies, then starts off again scenting the track of a victim. Soon it sees a covey of birds searching the ground for seeds and grubs. Sneaking downwind of them, the dog waits until one bird, unaware of danger, walks almost into its fangs. Although Azara's dog has the appearance of a fox, and it and others similar to it are often called South American foxes because of their pointed muzzles, pricked ears, short legs and long bushy tail, this animal is actually related to the wolf and jackal. It is rarely seen in the forests of Paraguay and Argentina, which are its true home, but it has an insatiable appetite for sugar cane and will leave its more protected haunts to raise havoc in the cane-fields, slashing and chewing the

stalks as if this were its last meal. Its normal diet, however, is birds, small mammals, snakes and lizards. Its shelter is often a burrow lately vacated by an armadillo.

BABOON

If a toad appears to have an over-weaning gluttony it is because it has neither the intelligence nor the capability for storing excess food. Higher in the animal scale, among birds and mammals, the hoarding of excess food is a marked feature of the animals' behaviour. A squirrel burying nuts is a typical example, but more intelligent was the stratagem used by a baboon.

Baboons live in troops and together they go out each day foraging, turning over the stones for insects and scorpions, and picking up any fruit grain or vegetables they may find. Where

Azara's dog *(Dusicyon azarae)*

Chacma baboon *(Papio ursinus)*

in Africa the ground is tilled they do enormous damage to the crops because these provide an easy living. A troop of baboons must always be on the look-out for enemies, so they try to obtain as much food as possible in the shortest time they can. In this they are assisted by their capacious cheek pouches, into which they can stuff food and carry off more than can be eaten on the spot.

A writer in *Scientific American* several years ago told how an old male **chacma baboon** increased the amount he could carry away. This old male lived on his own away from the troop. There were a number of leopards in the district and leopards are particularly fond of baboon. This old male baboon seemed to have been determined not to be caught napping when raiding the maize crops. He would bind a piece of rope or a vine around his middle and when he came to a field of maize or a place where it was stored he would push the cobs under his belt in case he had to leave in a hurry. On one occasion he ambushed two women who were on their way to market with baskets of the grain on their heads. The baboon stepped out on to their path, made terrifying noises and gestures at them so that they panicked and fled leaving the maize scattered on the path. The baboon collected this up and made off with it.

BABOON, CHACMA

Making tracks in the sand like those left by children playing, the **chacmas** search the parched landscape of South Africa and Bechuanaland for food and water. Although they are the largest baboons in the world and appear ferocious, they are not really predators. The humble ostrich egg is perhaps their favourite food. By just breaking off one piece of the shell they are able to drain its contents. Sifting the sand with their fingers can lead to other delicacies, like beetles and ant-lions. The iris bulb, on the other hand, is dug up, and when unearthed the chacma sits back and peels it like an orange. In their continual search for under-

Gelada baboon *(Theropithecus gelada)*

ground water, groups of as many as thirty baboons may combine. Even in the desert this pack will find the right spot to dig down. While they are about this task, however, someone must scan the horizons for their enemies, the prowling leopards. On high ground above the troop, at least two baboons will stand guard, and move their heads back and forth, more like a radar scanner.

Chacma baboon (*Chaeropithecus ursinus*)

BABOON, GELADA

A glance at the picture here will show what a formidable enemy the **gelada baboon** or "Dog Monkey", of Ethiopia, must be. The menacing fangs of the adult male are actually larger than those of a tiger, and his bristling mane gives him a battle-cloak at once protective and terrifying. Under this cloak is a naked pink chest. It is one of the strangest things to note how different is the young gelada. He is a pathetic-looking little creature, "gentle as a lamb", and with no indication of the hideous warrior he will become. Their food has to be wrested from the rocky ground, where they hunt for roots, tubers, seeds, leaves, fruit and small animal life. In addition to their threatening appearance and fearsome teeth, they will attack enemies by throwing stones or rolling rocks down the hillside.

BABOON, YELLOW

Forever seeming to bicker and argue amongst themselves, it is a wonder that the **yellow baboons** ever do get together for a raid. Yet, they are in full force, attacking an ostrich's nest and seizing her eggs, even before the helpless creature can gather her wits. When they have these large white globes in their hands, they crack them open and drain the yolks. The pack works together for many of its meals. Take insects, for instance. One of the baboons uproots a bush and beats it upon the ground. When all the insects fall off, the whole clan is there ready for the "pickings". If any berries drop at the same time, this is considered an added bonus. The three-foot-tall yellow baboon has a sweet tooth also, and throughout the open grasslands from Egypt to Rhodesia a pack can frequently be seen raiding a hive. By rolling the comb in the grass, they are able to free it of its stinging insects, and make it fit to eat.

Yellow baboon (*Chaeropithecus cynocephalus*)

BABOON, SACRED

It is a good job for the **hamadryas** that it has a small stomach, despite its Herculean chest measurements. Good because the rocks it lives among in barren regions of Arabia and of north-east Africa provide scanty nourishment. It has no specially "favourite" food because it has little choice. It must grub for roots, bulbs, underground insects, and seeds when it can find them. Fortunately there are also lizards sunning themselves, and some varieties of snails. Unlike many other baboons that are expert mountaineers, the hamadryas has legs and arms of about equal length, and they are more adapted to level ground than to swift climbing. It has fierce eyes and a pink face, but it takes no pride in them. The hamadryas seems to lead a morose kind of life, and is jealously watchful of the female members of his family. Taken early enough this baboon could be tamed, as its ancestors were in Ancient Egypt. Incredible as it may seem, these baboons were then trained to weed gardens, pick fruit, act as water carriers, and even to wait at table, so we are told. This is the baboon represented in Egyptian antiquities, and which is also known as the Sacred Baboon.

BABOON, SACRED

Among the many sacred animals of Ancient Egypt, baboons were specially consecrated to the god Thoth, to whom they were confidential counsellors. They are shown in sculptures,

Hamadryas or sacred baboon

(Papio hamadryas)

Hamadryas baboon

(*Papio hamadryas*)

usually sitting hands on knees, with their great manes spread around them like cloaks; awe-inspiring figures in magisterial postures. Indeed, they were so honoured that, like the Pharaohs and the greatest in the land, they were embalmed at death, and their mummies preserved in an imposing mausoleum in the city of Thebes. One sculptured bas-relief shows three baboons picking figs from a tree and putting the fruit into baskets held by slaves. These animals are known today as the **Hamadryas,** also as **Arabian** or **Sacred baboons,** living in Arabia and Ethiopia, on both sides of the Red Sea. They must have lost much of their sacred character to be employed as fruit-pickers. Some writers go further and say that the baboons were trained as helpers in the house, and to wait at table in the manner shown in the picture. It is of interest to note that to-day, thousands of years later, it is being seriously suggested that monkeys and apes should be tamed and set to work on menial tasks required by our modern civilization.

See Also: MONKEY

BACKSWIMMER

The total purpose of the **backswimmer's** existence is to kill. Sucking out blood from a small fish, it does not release its hold until the fish is dead. Its only weapon is its dagger-like beak which can puncture deep wounds. In ponds throughout the world its chief prey are

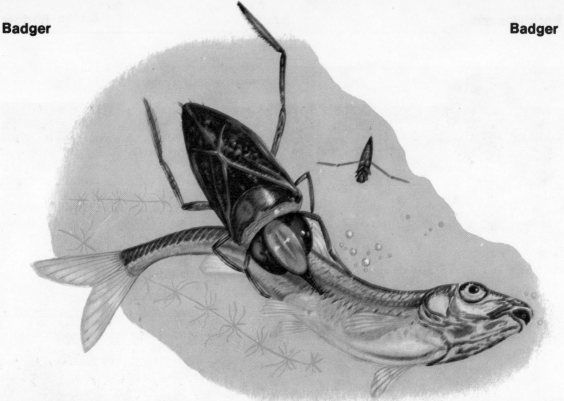

Backswimmer *(Notonecta maculata)*

smaller insects, and in its turn it is eaten by other water insects and by fish. Boat-shaped, it moves by propelling itself through the water with its long, oar-like hind legs, and because of this is known in Britain as the water-boatman. Backswimmer, the name used more in North America, is equally apt, for the insects floats and swims upside down. Being lighter than water, it has to grab hold of a plant stem or it would rise to the pond's surface. Yet, it must periodically float up for it needs air at all times Re-submerging, the backswimmer carries air-bubbles on its body's surface, trapped among the bristles on the body, as a man might carry an oxygen tank. Not confined only to the water, these insects can fly, so, if the pool dries up, they can find another one – even a long distance away.

BADGER, AMERICAN

The great plains of North America stretch from Canada to Mexico. Here the **American badger** makes its home. One of the largest of the burrowing mammals, it measures more than

three feet from the tip of its pointed nose to its skimpy tail. It has long claws and can dig down through the earth with amazing speed. Its deep burrows may reach more than thirty feet under ground. Here the female makes her nest and rears her young – usually five or six in each litter. The youngsters, like their parents, are born with a skin which is very loose, almost as if it were too large for them; but is very thick and tough. Protected by their heavy pelts and their fearless ways, the youngsters grow up in a world where they need fear few enemies except man. But the adult American badger is not without competition on the plains. The **coyote** hunts the same prey – the little prairie dogs that sit up like question marks beside their underground burrows. Although the coyote hunts over the plains, the American badger is so strong and so fierce that it seldom gives the wild dogs more than a passing glance. The American badger differs slightly from the European badger in appearance but it differs more in what it eats and in the way it digs. To begin with it goes more for rodents, such as pocket gophers and ground squirrels, in addition to prairie dogs. It will also kill and

American badger *(Taxidea taxus)*

Coyote *(Canis latrans)*

eat snakes and skunks, lizards and birds' eggs, but like the European badger it kills rabbits and is also fond of digging out nests of wild bees. Although its burrows may run thirty feet underground they are seldom more than six feet below the surface at their deepest point. This is where the sleeping chamber is and where the young are born, in a nest of dried grass. Except when it has young the American badger does not remain long in any one burrow, which is

markedly different from the European badger, who is faithful to the set, as the system of deep underground tunnels is called.

Once the American badger has scented a prairie dog or a pocket gopher it starts digging at the entrance of the rodent's burrow and bores down in a spiral at top speed. It digs so rapidly that it sometimes disappears below the surface, especially in soft earth, in a little more than a minute. It is a past master in the use of tunnels. In the northern parts of North America, for example, it may burrow below the frozen surface soil and plug up the entrance with a clod of earth to keep out the cold.

BADGER, AMERICAN

More truly carnivorous than its European cousin, the **American badger** digs deep holes when seeking out prairie dogs, ground squirrels and marmots. If hungry enough, it will even brave the odour and attack skunks. This fussy housekeeper never takes its meals indoors, for the bones of its victims would clutter the clean

American badger *(Taxidea taxus)*

Sand Badger (*Arctonyx collaris*)

house or "sett" it keeps freshly lined with dry grass and ferns. On the other hand, excess food is buried and later dug up to be eaten as needed. Apart from prairie dogs the American badger's diet includes a variety of rodents, birds and their eggs, lizards, snails, insects and carrion. Perhaps the main differences from the European badger, apart from its markings and more carnivorous ways, lie in the American badger's ability to dig. When surprised by an enemy in the open it will burrow so rapidly that the soil is thrown up as if it were a geyser.

BADGER, SAND

When the big white Oriental moon appears over the horizon, and most animals are settling to sleep, the day is just beginning for the thirty-inch-long grey **sand badger**. Awakening from sleep, he and his near-sighted mate sniff their way out of the cave home which they have skilfully fashioned for themselves among piles of rocks. During most of the night, the two dig for earthworms insects and roots, stopping

occasionally to gobble a small snake or a little bird. The long claws of the sand badger are perfectly suited to burrowing in the soil for its favourite foods, but its nose is even more valuable to it. Since it can neither see nor hear very well, the sand badger depends upon its long, sensitive snout to find its way around in its native India, Burma and China. If an enemy ventures near, up goes its antenna-like nose to check the danger, and in a moment the two peaceful sand badgers are scurrying back into their rocky home hidden among the long grass. This long snout has given the animal the alternative name of hog-badger. It is believed that, in addition to giving the animal an acute sense of smell, the snout is also used for rooting in the ground, as all members of the pig family do, for food. But although this badger ranges over a wide area in south-east Asia and most of China little is known of its habits because it comes out only at night and because it is so shy of human beings. It is also a savage and formidable animal at close quarters. It also gives out a most unpleasant odour.

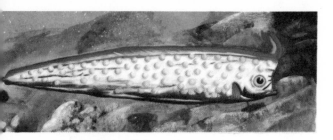

Crested bandfish (*Lophotus guntheri*)

BANDFISH

The rare **crested bandfish** of New Zealand is often called a Ribbonfish because of its elongated, ribbon-like body. It is one of the rarest of fish and very little is known of its habits. Occasionally washed up on beaches by storms, along with its relative, the Oarfish, it is quite possible that the crested bandfish is responsible for some of the sea-serpent stories. It can, however, be distinguished from other ribbon-like fishes by its peculiar forehead which is elevated, and slopes forward over its flat snout. A small mouth contains irregular teeth, and the eyes are round and large. It is said that whenever its body is touched, it erects the flag-like crest on the top of its head. Many taboos and superstitions are associated with this type of fish, but very little is known about the life history of this one.

BANDICOOT

As a result of ruthless killing the handsome **rabbit bandicoot** was exterminated in large parts of the Australian continent, and today is found only rarely in the south and south-west parts of the country. The **bilby,** as it is popularly called in Australia, is a long-eared creature and looks very much like a rabbit. Its tail, however, is long, and ends in a naked tip. The animal makes an interesting picture whilst sleeping; it sits up with its head tucked down onto its chest, in the manner of an old man sitting in a chair, who has just dropped off for forty winks. In the wild it hunts only at night and is made extremely uncomfortable

Rabbit bandicoot or bilby (*Thylacomys lagotis*)

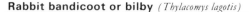

by the light. Out in the bush, the creature hides from the sun and from enemies, by burrowing long and maze-like tunnels in the earth with the very strong claws of its forefeet. The bilby will not only eat eggs but also will hunt any mammal smaller than itself, and captive rabbit bandicoots have rejected roots and fruit.

BANTENG

Lolling under a tree to escape the tropical sun is a common pose of the **banteng,** the only existing true species of wild cattle. Its native home is Java, although it was probably more widespread formerly in the south-east Asian region. Wherever dense growths of trees and underbrush cover a fairly large tract of rain-soaked land, the banteng can usually be found, travelling in small herds. Although placid by nature, there is fierce rivalry among male bantengs to dominate the herd, and after many battles the victor rules as chief. Little is known

Banteng *(Bos banteng)*

of the past history of this animal but it is thought by some scientists to be the wild stock from which the zebu, or Oriental domestic cattle, was derived.
See Also: ZEBU

BARBEL

Many a **common barbel** has ended its life swinging from the rod of a delighted angler. Found in rivers and lakes in Northern Italy and throughout France and Germany, this fish is considered to be particularly fine sport in England, where giants three feet long and weighing twenty pounds have occasionally been caught. As he patiently sits on the damp river bank awaiting a tug on his line, every angler must dream of catching a barbel of this size. The fish gets its name from the projections which grow down from his upper lip. Although they look somewhat like tusks, these barbs are quite soft and fleshy and are organs of touch, used for searching the river bottom in the

endless hunt for food. A member of a very large family, the common barbel's smaller and more brightly coloured relations are well known to miniature fish fanciers whose aquariums they grace. The continental barbel seem to go to a greater size than those in England. A weight of 33 lbs. has been recorded and it has been said that barbel in the Rhine and Danube may reach 50 lbs. weight.

Common barbel (*Barbus barbus*)
The barbel is a catfish. This group of fish are identified by the two to four pairs of catlike whiskers each fish has. Scientists call these whiskers barbels. This is also the word many Europeans use to identify the large catfish found in their waters.

BARBET

Some of the sites selected by birds for their nests may seem peculiar to us. With his mate the eight-inch **red-and-yellow barbet** of East Africa selects a very strange place – the inside of a towering termite mound in the hot, dry bush country. Having chosen the spot they begin industriously to hack with their heavy beaks into the side of the termite nest, while below there may be a family of dwarf mongooses living in a chamber at the bottom of the termitarium. For about a week, both the male and female red-and-yellow barbets chisel like woodpeckers into the termite dwelling, making their own tunnel and nest chamber amid the many galleries which honeycomb the sun-baked mud tower. There they settle down to raise their family, making daily trips to the surrounding bush to find their favourite fruits. Although the red-and-yellow barbets eat many insects, and feed their young on them, they never eat a single termite among the thousands which swarm about their strange home. Just why these bright-coloured birds leave the termites completely unharmed is another mystery, but there are many instances of a similar situation

which suggest that animals do not molest others living on their doorstep, even when they belong to the species they normally prey upon. See Also: SYMBIOSIS

Red-and-yellow barbet (*Trachyphonus erythrocephalus*)
Barbets make their nests in huge termite mounds. After the young hatch both mother and father will fly off frequently in search of food. And although they are surrounded by termites, barbets will not feed their young a single termite.

BARBFISH

The **barbfish** looks more like an armoured gladiator than a fish. One of the scorpionfishes, or mail-cheeks, its pugnacious appearance comes not least from the bony plate extending like a piece of armour from its eye to its gill. From its spiky appearance one would not think its flesh very good to eat, at one time any barbfish caught were thrown away.

Barbfish (*Scorpaena brasiliensis*)

Now it is fished with hook and line in rocky areas and by trawl-net in the open sea. Tremendously prolific, a foot-long female will give birth to twenty thousand live young at a time.

that other larvae swimming near are attracted to do likewise. It may be that the newly-settled larvae give off a chemical into the water which attracts other larvae. That we can only

BARNACLES

Barnacles are hard-shelled marine animals which live firmly attached to rocks, piers and ships, although when first hatched, the larval barnacles swim freely in the sea. There are two kinds, the stalked or **gooseneck barnacles** and the **acorn barnacles,** which are seated direct on the rock or ship's bottom, without a stalk. Both feed in the same way, by pushing out their bristly legs through an opening in the shell and waving them through the water to capture small animals or particles of food. To see the way barnacles are scattered all over the rocks on the seashore it looks as if the larvae just settle wherever they happen to fall. This is not the case. If the surface on which a larva has settled is not suitable it will, after exploring it for a while, swim away. Once a group has settled and turned into adult barnacles, it seems

Gooseneck barnacle (*Lepas anatifera*)
Acorn barnacle (*Balanus* sp.)

guess. The fact can be observed that they do settle in groups and seem to attract other larvae to do the same.

Although barnacles belong to the lower animals, they do seem to have a simple means of communicating with each other. The higher animals form associations, known as schools, shoals, herds or flocks, and these associations are formed and held together, as we have seen, by signals. These signals may be made through the use of the voice, the sounds be perceived through the ear, or they may be signals perceived through the eye or the nose. The lower animals cannot hear, and at best they have only simple eyes capable of no more than distinguishing the difference between light and darkness. They do not have a nose, as such. What they do have is a general chemical sense. This is not easy to understand because we ourselves are so accustomed to using special sense-organs: eyes, ears and nose. A chemical sense can be roughly described as a kind of simple taste and smell combined, but not necessarily located in any obvious sense-organs. In barnacles, however, the chemical sense resides in the antennae.

From their behaviour we get the impression that the larvae of other lower animals living in the sea behave as barnacle larvae do. That is, it seems that when a few have settled others swimming near sense their presence and settle in the same spot. There is an obvious advantage for the acorn barnacles, that the larvae should not merely settle at random. Were there no provision against this the losses among the larvae would be even higher than they are. The larvae settling on mud or sand would almost certainly be doomed. So there is a clear benefit in having larvae which do settle on a firm surface giving out into the water substances, in minute traces, which act as signals and, so to speak, draw other larvae swimming into the vicinity to settle beside them.

BARRACUDA

Life at sea holds few terrors for the merchant seaman equal to the shrill clanging of the ship's alarm and the cry – "Torpedo"! Beneath the surface of the ocean, the diver feels a similar cold thrill of fear when confronted by the torpedo-shaped outline of the **great barracuda.**

Great barracuda *(Sphyraena barracuda)*

Suspended ominously in the clear water, it does not stalk its prey but will attack anything that makes erratic movements – such as a wounded fish. Hunting alone or in packs, it is the most dangerous of its kind as well as the largest – it sometimes reaches a length of twelve feet, although six feet is more usual. Unlike a shark, it makes a single attack that leaves a clean wound with no jagged edges, but its jutting jaw with its fang-like teeth is capable of severing an arm. Arrowing through the water towards its target, impelled by the relentless drive of its hunger, the great barracuda is probably the most deadly submarine danger in the ocean.

It used to be said that sharks sever a man's limb in one bite. In recent years, there has been a great deal of research into the ways and habits of sharks, largely in an endeavour to devise methods of preventing attacks by sharks near bathing beaches. At the same time several books have been published giving their authors' researches into the case histories of people that have been injured by sharks. As a result of these researches it seems highly unlikely that a shark ever severs a limb, and that when a limb is found in a shark's stomach it is because the shark has come across a corpse in a state of decomposition so that the limb has come away naturally from the rest of the body. Attack by the great barracuda seems to be as vicious and as dangerous as that of any shark, and very often it is a matter for doubt whether the person who has been injured in the sea has been attacked by a shark or a barracuda. It does seem, however, that a large barracuda can in fact sever a limb with one snap of the jaws. Another feature of barracuda attack, which makes it a greater menace than attack by shark is that it may take place in much shallower water.

All this must sound very frightening, and there is no question that the barracuda must be treated with the greatest possible respect. Nevertheless, compared with the number of people that go bathing or skin-diving, barracuda attacks are much less frequent than attacks by sharks, and like shark attacks they occur only in the warmer waters.

See Also: SHARK

BARRIER REEF FISH

"More dangerous than sharks", is the verdict of divers exploring the crevices and caverns of Australia's Great Barrier Reef. This is the Queensland grouper, or **giant barrier reef fish,** whose inquisitiveness is as insatiable as its terrific appetite. It has been known to stalk a shell-diver as a cat stalks a mouse, and to make a rush with the full impetus of its quarter-ton weight. Australian newspapers report salvage-divers being repeatedly attacked by groupers attracted by the shiny helmets. One fish took a helmet in its mouth and made off, of course dragging the wearer with it. The man was rescued in the nick of time. Brisbane Marine Officials say: "It is thought that the mysterious loss of some native pearl divers is due to Groupers". This great fish is most often found lurking in deep valleys or old wrecks on the sea floor. It has a cavernous mouth, and this has given rise to legends of skin-divers being swallowed alive. Fortunately these are untrue, for the grouper's throat is not wide enough!

See Also: GROUPER

Basenji
Basenji have been used as hunters by the people of Central Africa for thousands of years.

BASENJI

A frightened antelope leaps from its hideout in the African bush, and crashes straight into a trap set by a hunting party of Congolese. What

Giant barrier reef fish *(Promicrops lanceolatus)*

alarmed the antelope and sent it fleeing from its place of safety? It was the din of stones rattling in gourds tied around the necks of a pack of small, chestnut-coloured **basenji** dogs. These fearless little dogs, from an ancient lineage native to the Congo River basin, also beat huge wild beasts out of the deep bush, using either clanging bells or the same gourds tied around their necks. The sixteen-inch high basenji has been known in Africa for more than four thousand years, as explorers have found in examining ancient Egyptian rock carvings. Although the local peoples there have used basenjis for centuries as hunting dogs, the outside world knew almost nothing about them until 1936, when five were taken to England. Its good manners, added to its comically wrinkled face and to the fact that it never barks, have endeared the basenji to many people in Europe as an affectionate and intelligent pet.

See Also: DOG, HUNTING

BASS

Of all the world's fish, whether in fresh or salt water, none leads a more desperate existence than the North American **large-mouth bass.** From the first independent swim after hatching, the young bass has to battle furiously for its life. Eat or be eaten is the law in its slow-moving rivers and green-margined lakes. The mouth of the youngster grows wider almost daily, graduating from snails, worms, crayfish, tadpoles and mice to the fully-grown large-mouth of two to three feet long which can engulf large frogs, rats, snakes, and even little ducklings unlucky enough to swim overhead. When he is guarding newly-hatched fry the male is ferocious enough to scare off even the largest enemies, except such a deadly foe as the otter. A more subtle enemy, against which he is powerless, is the tapeworm that attacks his reproductive organs, making him incapable of fertilising eggs. If it were not

Large-mouth bass *(Micropterus salmoides)*

for these, and other exterminators, the large-mouth bass would surely depopulate vast stretches of America's inland waters.

There are two kinds of fishes known as basses and although fairly closely related they belong to separate families. There are the sea basses and the freshwater basses of which the large-mouth bass is one of several species. The freshwater basses belong to the family known as the sunfishes. There is a sunfish living in the sea. The freshwater sunfishes have received their name because they react very quickly to sunshine. When the sun is shining they disperse and go about their original occupations but when a cloud obscures the sun they bunch together as though something had alarmed them.

The large-mouth bass does not behave in this way but it is included in the same family because its anatomy is like that of the typical sunfish. In fact the large-mouth bass behaves like a typical hunter. Although it will eat almost anything living that comes its way, its main food is other fishes and to catch these it lurks among the roots of water plants or between stones, and from its hide-out pounces on its prey as it passes.

As so often happens with a species that is highly predatory, the large-mouth bass is particularly belligerent towards others of its own species. One result of this is to keep the individual fishes spaced out, but the belligerence is especially marked during the breeding season. The male bass builds his nest and defends it and the territory immediately around it against all other males. Fights along the borders between the territories are quite common. However, should a female enter the territory he meets her with raised fins and after a brief courtship the two begin to circle inside the nest, she laying a few eggs at a time and he fertilising them. But the moment she has finished laying he drives her out.

Several females may lay in one nest, which may in the end contain up to 10,000 eggs.

BAT

Bats are the only true flying mammals. Only in the last quarter of a century has the secret been revealed about their hideous gargoyle faces, but they have been regarded with revulsion for thousands of years. In some places they can been seen pouring out of their roosts in the evening, like black clouds of smoke. They have long been regarded with superstitious fear, and were thought to be evil spirits fluttering up from the grave of the world. The truth is far more interesting. The bat known as the **flying fox** ranges over Asia and Australia, flying out

Flying fox *(Pteropus edulis)*

at sundown to feed on ripening fruit. Hanging upside down among the twigs, it drags the fruit to its mouth with its clawed hand. Its resemblance to a fox is startling, especially the small pricked ears, long muzzle and rich ruff of fur about the neck. Guided by an acute sense of smell it ravages fruit crops in forest and farm. The **noctule** of Europe is an insect-eater, often seen hunting with swifts at sunset. It has an audible high-pitched squeak and an

Noctule or great bat *(Nyctalus noctula)*

Barbastelle *(Barbastella barbastellus)*

Long-eared bat *(Plecotus auritus)*

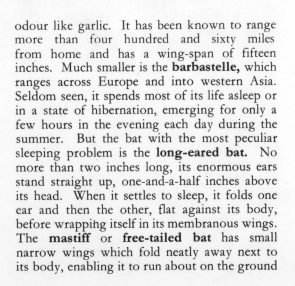

Mastiff or free-tailed bat *(Tadarida taeniotis)*

odour like garlic. It has been known to range more than four hundred and sixty miles from home and has a wing-span of fifteen inches. Much smaller is the **barbastelle,** which ranges across Europe and into western Asia. Seldom seen, it spends most of its life asleep or in a state of hibernation, emerging for only a few hours in the evening each day during the summer. But the bat with the most peculiar sleeping problem is the **long-eared bat.** No more than two inches long, its enormous ears stand straight up, one-and-a-half inches above its head. When it settles to sleep, it folds one ear and then the other, flat against its body, before wrapping itself in its membranous wings. The **mastiff** or **free-tailed bat** has small narrow wings which fold neatly away next to its body, enabling it to run about on the ground

on its four well-developed feet. The largest and strongest bat in North America, it has a dog-like face and short fur with a large tail and triangular ears that join across the top of its forehead. As is usual in bats, the large ears catch the echoes of the bats' high-pitched squeaks, guiding their owners towards flying insects or warning them of obstacles in their path.

BAT

It follows as a matter of course that, when speaking of sleep in animals, bats should receive the most attention. They sleep more than most animals and the way they do so is more varied than in any other group. Indeed,

Epauletted bat *(Epomophorus wahlbergi)*

The epauletted bat is a member of the fruit bat species. It is also closely related to the bats called flying foxes. The epauletted bat only eats fruit and flowers. It has large eyes and, unlike other bats, very sharp eyesight.

if other animals could be said to live to eat, bats could almost be said to live to sleep. Something of this idea could have been in the mind of the Roman author Lucanius who, according to the Italian naturalist, Ulysses Aldrovandus, writing in 1581, left us a description of the Island of Sleep. This island stood in the middle of a river named Nyctipotus, which being translated means Waters of Darkness. Its only inhabitants were bats.

We do not know where this island was located but it could stand for any one of a large number of islands in the tropics where fruit bats roost during the day. Some of these roosts are on actual islands in rivers and others are in islands of trees growing in grasslands. Both kinds can be found in Africa and also in southern Asia. The **epauletted bat** of West Africa is one species of fruit bat that behaves in this way, and its behaviour is typical of fruit bats as a whole.

At dusk the bats take off and fly in a body to some place where fruit is ripening, to gorge themselves. After this they return to their roost to settle on the upper branches of the trees where they hang, during the daylight hours, like monstrous fruits themselves. Through using one island of trees habitually the bats denude the branches in the upper part of the trees of foliage. This only makes more conspicuous the sleeping bats hanging by their hind-feet, and shading their eyes from the sun by the corners of their folded wings.

BAT

There is a second candidate, or, better still, group of candidates, for the title of the world's best sleepers. These are the insect-eating bats of the temperate latitudes of the

Serotine *(Eptesicus serotinus)*

northern hemisphere. It is, however, far from easy to deal with these in a cut-and-dried manner. Although bats are so familiar to everyone, and have been studied fairly closely by naturalists for over fifty years, it is only within the last twenty years that they have been studied at all intensively.

We could say, without risk of being too wide of the truth, that the northern insect-eating bats hibernate for half the year and spend half of each day during the remaining six months in a state resembling hibernation. Moreover, there are few bats that spend the whole of the night on the wing. Usually they hunt for short periods during the night and rest in between these flights. The amount of sleep they enjoy must cover somewhere in the region of 80 to 90 per cent of their total existence.

However, these remarks are no more than a generalization, and any generalization is an over-simplification. To offset this a few particular items of information must be included.

So far as the daily sleep is concerned we know that all bats so far studied behave in the same way. They stay in their roosts, which may be a hollow tree, cave, roof-space or tower, from dawn to dusk, approximately. In the roost they hang upside-down, suspended by the hook-like claws of their hind feet. While in this position their body temperature falls to that of the surrounding air, their rate of breathing drops and so does their pulse-rate. They are, therefore, in their daily sleep, in a state closely resembling that of typical hibernation. On awakening for their night's hunting they have to warm up, and these preliminaries include much wing-flapping and, in those bats occupying a roomy roost such as a roof-space, a certain amount of running around using wings and hind-legs in a quadrupedal manner.

Most bats sleep with the wings merely folded against the sides. The **horseshoe bats** are peculiar in that they hang freely suspended from a ceiling with their wings wrapped around the body, much as a person might wrap a cloak around his body against a cold wind. Even while speaking of bats sleeping throughout the daylight hours it must be remembered that such sleep is not necessarily unbroken. Some species, like the pipistrelle, creep so completely out of sight into cracks and crevices that it is hard to say what their daytime habits may be. Serotines are more obvious in their roosts and these we know will readily awaken at slight sounds and will look up to see what is afoot. A **serotine** may even scamper towards the source of a sound to find out what is happening.

Two species of bats that have been fairly fully investigated in England are the serotine and the greater horseshoe bat. The serotine hunts periodically throughout the night. Its first flight lasts for about 45 minutes after which it returns to its roost to rest. Its prey is mainly moths, and on warm nights, when moths are flying well, it may make three or more such sorties in a night. In October, about the third week, it goes into hibernation and it sleeps solidly, so far as we can tell, until late April or early May.

The greater horseshoe bat also goes to its winter quarters in late autumn but continues to hunt until about mid-December. From January onwards its feeding flights grow fewer, and hibernation then becomes more pronounced until the end of April. Even during this period, however, the sleep is anything but unbroken. The bats wake up and move around at intervals of a few days, and banding has shown that some individuals may make long flights. Flights of 15 miles have been recorded, and as much as 40 miles has been noted.

It has been suggested that this frequent

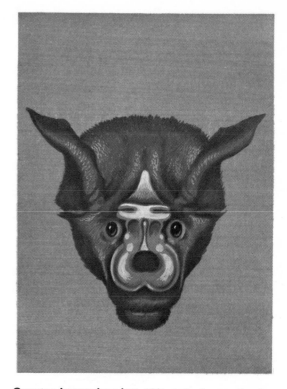

Greater horseshoe bat (*Rhinolophus ferrumequinum*)

The winter temperatures can cause the greater horseshoe bat to go into semi-hibernation. Though it sleeps as much as possible during cold weather, it does not hibernate totally.

interruption of the winter sleep by the horseshoe bat is due to the need to drink frequently to avoid drying up. That is, however, no more than a guess. The important point to emerge from the comparison of the habits of serotines and horseshoe bats is that, at the moment, we can only generalize widely about the sleeping habits of bats. Probably every one of the scores of species in the temperate regions of the northern hemisphere has its peculiar habits. What does emerge also is that bats, as a class, spend a high percentage of their lives asleep, or in a state of torpor, whichever is the more appropriate word to use in their case. This may account for the long lives they enjoy, up to 27 years or more, which is a very long life-span compared with other small mammals.

BAT, BANANA

There are about forty species of pipistrelle bats in the world, in North America, and in all continents of the Old World. They all have similar habits in that they appear on the wing fairly early in the evening and fly over a regular beat with a characteristic fluttering flight on a jerky and erratic course. They roost in crevices in hollow trees, among rocks, in caves or in buildings. Most of them, especially those in the colder parts of their range, use one roost in summer and another in winter, but usually they are fairly faithful to one particular roosting place during the course of a season.

The **banana bat,** a species of pipistrelle living in southern and eastern Africa, is forced to

change its roost from time to time because it chooses dried and rolled up banana leaves in which to sleep. The bat is able to do this because the soles of its hind feet form suction pads for clinging to the surface of the leaf.

Daubenton's bat (*Myotis daubentoni*)

BAT, DAUBENTON'S

One of the more common bats in the British Isles is **Daubenton's bat,** but it is also found over most of Europe and across Asia to Japan. It measures less than two inches from its muzzle to the tip of its tail, and its wing-span is just under ten inches, but it is so expert in flight that it can skim the surface of a river without wetting its wings, and fly so close that it is difficult to distinguish between the bat and its reflection in the water. Unlike larger bats which fly over long distances with a slow and measured stroke, Daubenton's bat moves its wings so rapidly that it seems to vibrate over the water. Often seen in large groups over the dark mirror of a lake – some pausing to drink while others scoop up water insects – these

Banana bat (*Pipistrellus nanus*)

Banana bat (*Pipistrellus nanus*)

little bats seem literally to float in the air, but they never collide in the darkness, no matter how closely they crowd together.

BAT, FLAT-HEADED

Some years ago, when workmen were demolishing a building, they had to break a hollow block of concrete. As the concrete fell apart a bat flew out and the story was that the bat must have somehow become incarcerated many years before, when the building was first constructed. Probably there is a simpler answer: that there was a crack somewhere in the concrete, large enough for a bat to creep in. It is surprising how small a space, between tiles, or in brickwork, is sufficient to allow a bat to insert itself. But the palm for this goes to a bat living in Malaya.

This is the **flat-headed bat,** which habitually roosts in the hollow stems of large bamboo. In one section of the bamboo there may be one or a small group of these bats that have crept in through a crack in the stem. The head, with the skull, is the least compressible part of an animal's body, and it is a popular saying that if an animal can get its head through a hole it will be able to squeeze the rest of its body through. This bat, having a flattened head, has a great advantage over other bats, in squeezing through cracks and using bamboos for its roost.

One other thing is needed. Even the flat-headed bat is unable to fly straight through the crack. It must land on the bamboo stem, the slippery surface of which offers little foothold. The flat-headed bat surmounts this difficulty by virtue of the suction pads on its feet, which enable it to cling to the edges of the crack while insinuating its body through it.

Flat-headed bat *(Tylonycteris pachypus)*

BAT, FLOWER-FACED

Of the one thousand or so species of bats in the world, probably one of the most grotesque in appearance is the **flower-faced bat** of the

Flower-faced bat *(Anthops ornatus)*

Solomon Islands. Suddenly this light, ugly flyer looms out of the semi-darkness, floating through the air and looking like something from a hideous nightmare. But apart from the large petal-like skin flaps surrounding its small face, which resemble two huge deformed ears on a tiny head, it is no worse than other bats; and it is not half so bad as it looks. These rosettes of skin, and the three ball-topped stems rising from them, are probably part of the direction-finding echo-location device with which all bats are equipped and which is truly one of the wonders of nature, enabling a bat not only to find its food but, on receiving back sound reflections of its own squeaks from a few inches ahead, to alter course instantaneously.

The flower-faced bat is an insect-eater and generally lives alone in a tree hollow.

BAT, FLOWER

The **long-tongued flower bat** is a native of the West Indies and feeds on fruit and flower pollen. Like many leaf-nosed bats, it has a tongue which can be thrust far out of its mouth like a slender stalk. At the tip of this remarkable tongue there is a pad of thread-like barbs. Once it was thought that these barbs were used to lick the skin off a victim before sucking its blood. Actually, it uses the barbs on its tongue to extract the pollen from flowers and the soft pulp from within tender-skinned berries. Its tongue is, in fact, so sensitive that it can lick

Long-tongued flower bat
(Phyllonycteris sezekorni)

the skin off a berry, and, in captivity, has been seen to lick a man's fingers clean of berry juice – even from beneath the finger nails. The long-tongued flower bat also has very long "thumbs" which it uses to turn berries and other tiny fruit around and around until all the rich pulp is gone – cleaned off by this slender, rasping tongue. Not even a hummingbird has so versatile a tongue as this small flying mammal.

Tube-nosed fruit bat *(Nyctimene* sp.*)*

BAT, FRUIT

Not horrifying like the hammer-headed bat but certainly ugly enough, is the **tube-nosed fruit bat,** with its blunt muzzle, and mouth like a zipped-up purse. The oddest things about it are the tubes which appear to have been stuffed up its nostrils. They project quite a distance, and set a puzzle till we find that the bat eats juicy fruits while hanging head downwards. In that position there would be the danger of juices trickling into or flooding the nasal cavities. But the tube extensions keep the nose, as one might say, "above water". They also prevent pollen dust from entering, for the tube-nosed fruit bat feeds on pollen too, as well as on some insects. Possibly the small lobes on the lips assist in holding insects. Another feature is its tail, which is nearly equal to the length of its lower leg. Although there are more than two hundred kinds of fruit bats, the tube-nosed bat is quite distinctive. There are a dozen species distributed over northern Australia and the islands off Malaya.

Hammer-headed bat (*Hypsignathus monstrosus*)

BAT, HAMMER-HEADED

Not many bats would get a vote in a beauty contest if the judges were human. In fact nearly all bat faces are ugly. But for sheer hideousness the male **hammer-headed bat** is unique. He is like a caricature of a horse's head set on a bat's body the head being so heavy that it hangs clumsily down when the creature is in flight. Seen in profile, the ears, eyes and muzzle are startlingly like those of a horse, but the big shock comes when viewing it from the front. We then see that the muzzle appears to have been chopped open, leaving flaps and folds too repulsive for words. Since the hammer-headed bat lives only in West Africa, one would think that he had been designed by a witch-doctor as a symbol of evil. In fact, he is quite inoffensive; he is only one of the fruit bats – and doubtless if a hammer-headed bat could express an opinion we should find he regarded men as ugly.

BAT, HARE-LIPPED

During last century a curious naturalist, a Professor M'Carty, visited the home of the **hare-lipped bat** which was located in a cave, seven feet from the water's edge along the Ecuador coast. As it was night-time he was not absolutely certain what they were doing gliding over the water's edge in such a manner. The scientist was able to capture several of them as they were about to re-enter their cave, then with the aid of a light he found the chewed remains of several fish within the creatures' stomachs. The bats were fishermen! The hare-lipped bat is a weird-looking predator that dwells in many parts of tropical America, from Mexico to Argentina. Its name comes from its upper lip, bent upwards to form an upside

Hare-lipped or bulldog bat (*Noctilio leporinus*)

down V. In general, the features of the head are not unlike those of a rodent. Our flying mammal makes good use of its claws as it glides over the surface of the water in a manner of a low-level bomber. During these raids it will bring up any dweller of the sea, from crustaceans to fishes twice its own weight. One must not assume, however, that our bat friend's diet is confined solely to seafood, for it will fly over dry land also and has been known to catch tree frogs, mice and even smaller bats.

BAT, HORSESHOE

There are more than a hundred species of **horseshoe bats** spread over wide areas of the globe, excepting the Americas. They are small, measuring on average about three and a quarter inches from nose to tail, with a hairless patch of skin on the upper lip shaped like a lucky horseshoe. Those known by the Latin name *Rhinolophus* are the most typical, in that the ears are long, wide and deeply cupped. Unlike many other bats, they tend to lead solitary lives, sleeping alone or roosting with only half a dozen others. Its roost may be in the attic

Greater horseshoe bat *(Rhinolophus ferrum-equinum)*

of a house, a hollow tree, or in the shade of spreading palm fronds. At dusk it flies around in search of insects, using its horseshoe charm, which for the insects it catches is always an unlucky charm. For a long time the purpose of this horseshoe was unknown. It is, in fact, a sensitive cup of skin, the margins of which can be raised and lowered to pick up echoes of the

Lattice-winged bat *(Centurio senex)*

bats' own squeaks, and is used for direction-finding.

BAT, LATTICE-WINGED

There lives in the Island of Trinidad a bat known as the **lattice-winged bat.** It has a wing span of about 12 inches, is light brown in colour with a white spot on each shoulder. It flies with a jerky butterfly movement with its body held vertical so that the wings are clearly seen as it flies about. These wings are marked with alternating bands of thick and thin skin, the thick bands appearing dark and the thin bands appearing light. This causes a kind of venetian blind effect.

Another unusual feature is that when the bat is asleep it covers its face with another kind of blind. Under its chin is a fold of skin which the bat is able to pull up over its face, past the mouth, the nose and the eyes to the top of the head, where there is a small knob that holds the flap in position. This holds the skin taut forming a kind of mask. The skin is hairy except for two patches of thin bare skin, and when the blind is pulled over the face these bare patches are located over the eyes. They are semi-transparent and they enable the bat to distinguish light from darkness. They also enable the bat to detect the shadow of an approaching object falling across them. This shadow may be from a passing animal that is unlikely to molest the bat, or it may be the shadow of an enemy coming in to attack. At all events, the bat takes no chances, quickly

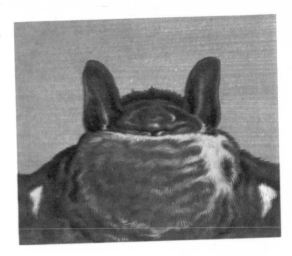

Lattice-winged bat *(Centurio senex)*

drops its mask to take a closer look, and if its fears are unfounded it pulls back the mask and continues its slumber.

BAT, LATTICE-WINGED

In Trinidad lives the **lattice-winged bat,** so-called because clear bands of skin in the wings produce a lattice-like effect. A lattice is, strictly speaking, a kind of network and it would be more appropriate to call this bat a lattice-mouthed bat because of the remarkable filtering apparatus on its lips. However, the filter does not stop there and in considering the whole of the bat's apparatus we have a most remarkable example of an animal that feeds on soft fruit pulp and juice using a natural suction and filter.

This bat, which has one of the ugliest faces of a group of animals noted for their ugly faces, is otherwise quite harmless, except to crops of fruit. It feeds on the over-ripe and mushy parts of bananas and paw-paws, and although it has teeth these are not as strongly developed as in other bats. These weak teeth may possibly be used for tearing open the fruit, although nobody has seen them do this, but they could equally well be used as strainers to supplement those on the lips. The skin between the bat's lips and gums is covered with numerous fleshy papillae. A papilla might be best described as a conical

pimple and it seems fairly certain that the bat sucks fruit juice or mushy pulp through the half-closed mouth with the papillae straining off any large pieces.

The bat's throat is extremely tiny, no more than one twelfth of an inch across. Since the bat itself has a wing-span of about 12 inches and a head the size of a ping-pong ball, this is a very, very small throat indeed. Behind this throat opening the gullet leads backwards but has a second opening of about the same size, and behind this second opening is a kind of bag leading out from the wall of the gullet which seems to act as a kind of sucking apparatus.

Some people advocate that to keep healthy we should chew all our food until it is almost liquid. The lattice-winged bat, instead of keeping a good set of teeth such as most bats possess, has in an evolutionary sense allowed its teeth to become weak and has gone to the trouble of developing a quite remarkable apparatus to ensure that its food is liquidized before it reaches the stomach. Whenever we find a peculiar structure of this kind in an animal we always find, once enough is known about the animal's way of life, that there is a very good reason for it. So far as the lattice-winged bat is concerned we do not yet know why it has developed this liquidizer. It may be that this is the quickest way it can take in sufficient food during the short time it is active each night.

Long-nosed bat *(Leptonycteris nivalis)*

that the long-nosed bats fed on nectar and pollen using their bottlebrush tongue to draw these substances into the mouth. It was, however, not suspected how large a quantity they consumed. It is only in the last few years that a more careful study has been made of these bats by examining them when they return to their roost after a feeding session. Then it was found that their stomachs were so distended with nectar that the skin of their belly was almost transparent through being stretched. The investigator reported that when he obtained a bat that had returned fatally injured to the roost, he found that the stomach was so distended with the clear nectar that he could read newsprint through the wall of the stomach and the enclosed nectar. It was rather like looking at a newpaper through one of those old-fashioned glass water bottles.

This particular bat had been injured by the spines of the cactus, and the same investigator reported that such injuries are not infrequent. Although the bats visit the flowers, push their heads into the blossoms and even grasp the petals with their toes, they do so with such a light touch that it is impossible to detect any injury to the petals. They use a similar skill in avoiding the cactus spines yet in spite of this they do sometimes impale themselves on the spines, so that they have to tug themselves free and then fly away with what may be a fatal stab.

BAT, LONG-NOSED

There is another kind of bat in the New World which also takes in liquid food but ha⁻ an entirely different method of doing so. This is the **long-nosed bat** living in the south-west of North America, from Arizona to Guatemala. It not only has a long nose but it also has a long tongue the outer half of which bears bristles, so that it resembles to some extent a bottle-brush. When feeding this bat visits the flowers of the saquaro cactus and also the one known as the shin-dagger cactus. Sometimes it starts at the top of a head of blossom and travels downwards, clinging to it and pushing its head first into one flower and then into another. At other times it may hover in front of a flower for a second or two as it pushes its head into the blossom. In this second case it looks exactly like a hummingbird and in fact what is happening is that the hummingbird feeds on the nectar and pollen of flowers by day and the long-nosed bat feeds on these same substances by night. Both of them not only obtain their food from the flowers but also carry the pollen on their heads from one blossom to another thus pollinating them. It always has been assumed

BAT, MOUSE-EARED

There are many other remarkable methods of feeding used by bats in different parts of the

Mouse-eared bat *(Myotis myotis)*

world, although the great majority merely catch insects on the wing. From time to time, however, somebody reports having seen one of these insect-eating bats on the ground and there has been a certain amount of speculation, as well as a slight mystery, about what it was doing there. A few years ago a German scientist looked into this and found that the **mouse-eared bat** in early spring has its stomach filled with 50 per cent of flying insects and 50 per cent of insects that live on the ground, such as beetles and caterpillars as well as some spiders. We know that when bats are pursuing winged insects they follow them with the aid of their echo-location. The question arises, however, by what means the bat decides when it overtakes the insect whether it is one it would wish to eat. We have no firm evidence on this point but it is a reasonable assumption that while the bat may pursue its prey by echo-location it must use its sense of smell at the last moment to decide whether to snap the insect up or not. Since the mouse-eared bat is now known to pursue insects on the ground we can be a little more sure on this point. It seems that they can

hear an insect moving over the ground provided it is not more than two inches from it, but the insect may be a dung beetle, which the bat eats, or it may a leaf-beetle, which the mouse-eared bat rejects. The assumption is that it uses the sense of smell to discriminate between desirable and undesirable insects, because it has been seen to push its nose into a clump of moss in order to capture a dung beetle, rather in the way that a dog will push its nose into the herbage in order to scent out a rabbit.

BAT, PROBOSCIS

One of the most extraordinary and co-ordinated sleeping habits is found in the **proboscis bat** of tropical America. The bat is grey and brown, with grey tufts on the fore-arms. It roosts by day in small companies of a score or so, each bat clinging by all four limbs, one in front of the other, fairly evenly spaced along the underside of a branch or a tree trunk overhanging a river. The colour

Proboscis bat *(Rhynchonycteris naso)*

of their fur gives them a resemblance to lichens, so that they are inconspicuous so long as they are still. Yet despite the protection of their camouflage as well as the security afforded by their choice of roosting site over water, they readily take wing when approached, all flying off together, the whole company acting as one unit, and landing again on a fresh roosting place in unison and in the same orderly formation.

BAT, MOUSE-TAILED (PYRAMID)

Bats are different from any other mammal in using true flight. They fly by virtue of having very long fingers with a membrane stretched across them. In becoming aviators there have been many and vast changes in their bodies. As a rule, when animals show evidence of great changes we can trace how these started and what course they have taken by studying the fossil remains of their ancestors. With bats it is different. Fossils of bats have been found, some of them dating back 50 million years or so. But even the earliest of these are already bats. So we have to speculate on how they came to look and behave as they do today. We can suppose that, in the first place, certain shrew-like animals, living in trees, took to leaping

from branch to branch. Then came changes in their bodies. The toes on the front legs grew long bones, and a membrane of skin was developed stretching between these long toes (or fingers, since they are on the front limbs). There is just a little evidence for this shrew-like ancestry in bats living today, in the **mouse-tailed bats** of the Middle East. They have tails longer than their bodies, which is what we may suppose their shrew-like ancestors had, whereas most bats living today have very short tails.

Pyramid bat *(Rhinopoma microphyllum)*

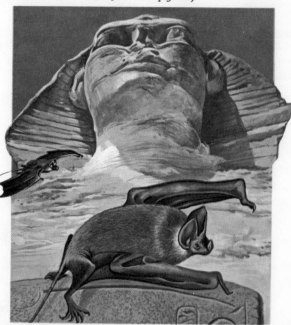

Mouse-tailed (Pyramid) bat *(Rhinopoma microphyllum)*

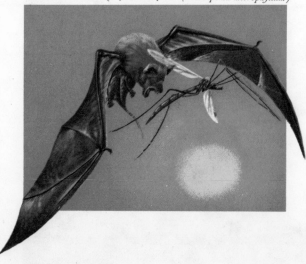

BAT, PYRAMID

The two archaeologists slowly move the final stone to open the Egyptian tomb. They jump back, startled... "It's the Pharaoh's curse!" A huge black cloud billows from the newly-excavated tomb. But they are not evil spirits, they are swarms of bats, including the one known as the **pyramid bat,** that find in the ancient monuments in Egypt a perfect dry

American red bat (*Lasiurus borealis*)

roost. They have every right to such ancient abodes, although where they roosted before the pyramids were built is another matter. Fossils of bats have been found that date back fifty-five million years, and they have changed their form hardly at all in that time. With most animals we can, by tracing back their fossil history, show how they came to have the form they have today. We can see what changes have taken place, and from what other kind of animal they have been derived. The ancestry of the bats can only be guessed. The pyramid bat uses its sonar system, listening to the echoes of the high-pitched sound it emits, to pin-point obstructions. This is how bats manage to live with up to twenty million fellow bats in one cave, as they do in the Carlsbad Caves of North America, without continually colliding one with the other.

BAT, RED

The **red bat** is found in southern Canada and the United States during the summer months. The most common of American bats, it sleeps during the day hanging among leaves, especially of oaks, and emerges at dusk to hunt for insects. At the first nip of autumn, however, the red bat forsakes this lonely way of life and, joining a small flock of its fellows, heads south towards Central America and the West Indies. These flocks, sometimes consisting solely of males or of females, fly on a steady course in contrast to the darting, swooping flight that they use when hunting insects. With its narrow tapering wings the red bat is, for its size, a flying machine of great speed and endurance. The mother bat bears two to four babies at a time, which she carries about for the first part of their life, their combined weight exceeding her own, a payload which must be the envy of every airline operator.

BAT, STRAW-COLOURED

Another fruit bat that roosts on islands is the **straw-coloured bat**. It is the fruit bat most widely distributed over Africa south of the Sahara and is noted for the way it moves about over long distances as the various fruits

Straw-coloured bat (*Eidolon helvum*)

ripen. It also eats the blossoms of some trees, even the young shoots of some of them, and will chew the soft wood of one palm, apparently to obtain moisture.

This bat is strongly gregarious and at its roost, in daytime, is often noisy and restless. It seems likely that the sounds made by this bat at roost are directed at preventing its fellows from hanging too near to it. So, in spite of their liking company, straw-coloured bats also like to be evenly spaced out.

One of the favoured foods of this bat is dates, and at times so much of this fruit is eaten that measures need to be taken against it to protect the crop. On the other hand, in the Congo, where they roost in the trees on islands in the Aruwimi River, the local peoples wade across at low water to kill them in large numbers for food. Both the nuisance value of the straw-coloured bat and its value as a source of food can be understood by the numbers found at roosts. Some roosts may have only a hundred or two bats, but other roosts may contain as many as ten thousand.

BAT, VAMPIRE

Blood. More blood every night, fresh from the living bodies of human beings or of beasts! This is the unceasing demand of the **vampire bat,** which takes no other food. How it obtains its ghoulish feasts reads like a horror story. It waits until its prey is asleep, drops close by, folds its leathery wings, and runs the remaining distance on all fours, like a huge hairy spider. Or it may run over the back of a large animal. With its sharp incisor teeth it makes a downward slash on the skin, so expertly that the victim does not wake. Then the vampire puts its lips to the base of the wound and laps up the flowing blood as a cat laps milk, so it is, strictly speaking, wrong to call it a bloodsucker. Men, horses, and practically all animals down to toads pay their blood tribute to the vampire bat. Sensational tales of a vampire gradually draining away the life's blood of a beautiful girl are physically impossible. These belong to a large fictional bat. The true vampire is only three and a half

Vampire bat (*Desmodus rotundus*)

inches long.   Even if it returned night after night it could not take away sufficient blood to cause illness or death.   The real danger is that the bat may be a carrier of the virus of a disease called derriengue, a kind of rabies which has often proved fatal to man and cattle in Mexico, Central America and Trinidad.

The vampire bat is the most specialized of all bats.   Its upper incisor teeth number only two and they have sharp chisel-like edges. Since it feeds on blood other teeth are unnecessary, and its cheek-teeth are minute.

BAT, FALSE VAMPIRE

The **false vampire bat** is a most unusual and ghastly looking creature.   Species of false vampires are found throughout much of Asia and Africa, even to Australia.   The bat's ears, meeting together above the head, are very large, several times the size of the face.   Two smaller ears seem to grow inside.   These are the earlets.   The nose looks more like a joke as it resembles two leaves, a smaller one placed on top of another one.   There are no upper incisors but twenty-eight sharp teeth still fill the mouth.   Having no visible tail their total length is a mere three inches, but the wing span can reach a foot and a half.   The false vampire bat is not a blood-sucker at all, although this used to be its reputation, but a true eater of flesh.   A Mr. Blyth reported seeing one of these creatures enter his house in India carrying a smaller bat in its mouth, which it dropped instantly when the man chased it.   At first this appeared to be a vampire's attack, for the captured one was weak from loss of blood. The truth was only brought to light in the morning when it was placed in the cage with its captor, who promptly ate it.   However, false vampires also feed on frogs, rodents and birds, as well as insects and other small animals.

False vampire bat *(Megaderma spasma)*

Yellow-eared bat *(Uroderma bilobatum)*

BATS, TENT-BUILDING

In 1888 a naturalist in Borneo reported having found nests made of moss by bats living in the caves there. There can be little doubt that what he saw were nests made by swifts, and there is no known instance of a bat having built a nest. There are, however, some bats that make a kind of tent or penthouse, by biting through the large broad leaves of tropical trees in Central America. One of them, the **yellow-eared bat** was first found sheltering in this way as recently as 1932. Nobody has ever caught it in the act of making its shelter but it is clear that the bat cuts across the leaf, about halfway along its length, so that the outer half bends down at

Watson's leaf-nosed bat *(Artibeus watsoni)*

A bat's palm-frond penthouse

Leaf cut to form a shelter

Leaf spread out to show line of cuts

an angle. The males rest singly under these shelters but the females with their young are found in groups. When disturbed at their roosts the bats fly swiftly and without hesitation to leaves on other trees that have been similarly cut through.

A palm with large fan-like leaves has been introduced into Panama, the home of the yellow-eared bat. This is also used, although the work of biting through the numerous folds of the palm leaves must require more skill.

In the same region lives a second species, **Watson's leaf-nosed bat,** which also cuts through palm leaves to make a penthouse roost.

BAT, WHISKERED

It is always supposed that the commonest bat in Europe is the pipistrelle but it is likely that the title of "common bat" should be shared by the whiskered. Certainly this is the more widespread. It is found throughout Europe, including the British Isles, across Asia even to Japan and southwards to parts of India, and it extends into Malaya and as far east as Sumatra, Java and Borneo.

One reason why the **whiskered bat** is apt to be overlooked is that it is mainly solitary, especially at its roosts. Sometimes a colony is found roosting together, but usually whiskered bats sleep in almost any place that will give them shelter, such as in roof-spaces, behind shutters or sign-boards, in holes in walls or in trees. They may sleep in ivy or in the spaces between boulders. Their wide choice of roosting places suggests that, unlike most bats which faithfully return to the same roosts day after day, the whiskered bat changes its doss-house fairly frequently.

The idea gains from what is known of the behaviour of whiskered bats in Malaya, which sleep in rolled up banana leaves. When the young leaves of the banana first appear they are rolled, just as you might pick up a sheet of notepaper and roll it round your fiinger. It is not unusual to find a whiskered bat asleep in one of these banana leaves. But soon after the young leaf has appeared it un-

folds and its fronds remain spread. Then the bat that has slept in it must find another roosting place, either another young banana leaf or a hole or cavity similar to it. To say the least, the mere fact that the whiskered bat should use the banana leaves in this way means that it is something of a nomad so far as sleeping quarters are concerned.

Whiskered bat (*Myotis mystacinus*)

BATFISH

The **batfish,** like a Spanish fan in shape and size, and sometimes called a fanfish, is a close relative of the ribbon fishes, and found in the same general area, around New Zealand. This fish, a foot or so long, brings with it a mystery which naturalists have not yet solved: most of the fish so far caught were found in the Cook Strait, the narrow stretch of sea between the North and South Islands of New Zealand. All the fish were mature females heavy with eggs, and it has been suggested that their repeated presence in Cook Strait means that they go there for a special reason, perhaps to breed. The indications are that this is a fish of the open

Batfish

oceans which is very seldom seen or caught alive. Even such specimens as have been found have mainly been washed ashore, and are always damaged.

See Also: BANDFISH

BATFISH, TORPEDO

Looking like a flying saucer from another planet, the ugly, flattened **torpedo batfish** slowly makes its way along the sea-bed off Hawaii. It proceeds in a kind of waddle using the arm-like pectoral fins as the main means of propulsion. To add to the resemblance to a flying saucer, it shoots twin spouts of water from its gill-chambers, at the rear of its two-inch body, like the exhaust of a jet aircraft. A batfish is one of the most awkward swimmers in the sea, and its shape is clearly an adaptation to life on the sea-floor. It is related to angler-fishes, which capture their prey with a rod and lure situated on the head. The torpedo batfish is provided with a built-in fishing rod, normally hidden in a little tube just above its mouth. When hungry, it shoots out this rod and waggles it causing the little

Batfish *(Halieutaea maoria)*

fleshy lure at its end to waggle, like a fisherman angling for a big fish. As soon as an inquisitive fish paddles up to examine the lure, the torpedo batfish snaps up its victim, and so swiftly that the action cannot be followed with the eye.

See Also: ANGLER

Torpedo batfish *(Halieutaea retifera)*